Superstars
of the
INDIANAPOLIS
COLTS

by Matt Scheff

amicus
high interest

Amicus High Interest is published by Amicus
P.O. Box 1329, Mankato, MN 56002
www.amicuspublishing.us

Library of Congress Cataloging-in-Publication Data
Scheff, Matt.
 Superstars of the Indianapolis Colts / Matt Scheff.
     pages cm. -- (Pro sports superstars)
 Includes index.
 ISBN 978-1-60753-526-3 (hardcover) -- ISBN 978-1-60753-556-0 (eBook)
 1. Indianapolis Colts (Football team)--History--Juvenile literature.
 2. Football players--United States--Biography--Juvenile literature. I. Title.
 GV956.I53S34 2014
 796.332'6409772--dc23
                          2013006839

Photo Credits: Damian Strohmeyer/AP Images, cover; David Drapkin/AP
Images, 2, 21; David Stluka/AP Images, 5; AP Images, 6, 9, 13; NFL Photos/
AP Images, 10; Scott Boehm/AP Images, 14; G. Newman Lowrance/AP
Images, 17, 22; Damian Strohmeyer/AP Images, 18

Produced for Amicus by The Peterson Publishing Company
and Red Line Editorial.

Editor Jenna Gleisner
Designer Becky Daum
Printed in the United States of America
Mankato, MN
2-2014
PO1197
10 9 8 7 6 5 4 3

TABLE OF CONTENTS

MEET THE INDIANAPOLIS COLTS

The Colts started in Baltimore, Maryland, in 1953. They moved to Indianapolis in 1984. The Colts have won four **NFL titles**. They have had many great stars. Here are some of the best.

GINO MARCHETTI

Gino Marchetti was a great **tackler**. It took at least two men to block him. He hit hard. He went to 11 **Pro Bowls** in a row! His first was in 1955.

RAYMOND BERRY

Raymond Berry was great at running the ball. He only **fumbled** one time in 13 seasons. He played his best in the big games.

Berry made the 1950s All-Decade team.

9

JOHNNY UNITAS

Johnny Unitas was one of the best passers of all time. He was a great leader, too. He won three **MVP** awards. He helped the Colts win the NFL title in 1958 and 1959.

Unitas helped the 1970 Colts win the Super Bowl.

JOHN MACKEY

John Mackey was a great **tight end**. He was big and fast. He caught a long pass in the 1971 Super Bowl. It was a 75-yard pass. It scored the Colts a touchdown.

14

MARVIN HARRISON

Marvin Harrison caught more passes than any other Colt. He helped the Colts win a Super Bowl. He was picked to play in eight Pro Bowls.

Harrison caught 143 passes in 2002. That is an NFL record.

PEYTON MANNING

Peyton Manning is smart. He has a strong arm. He led the 2006 Colts to a Super Bowl win. He also won four MVP awards with the Colts.

Manning's brother Eli plays for the New York Giants.

17

REGGIE WAYNE

Reggie Wayne knows how to get open. He can go deep. He catches a lot of passes. He had the most catches in the 2011 Pro Bowl. He has gone to six Pro Bowls.

ANDREW LUCK

Andrew Luck is a smart **quarterback**. He was a **rookie** in 2012. He led the Colts to the playoffs. He has a bright future.

The Colts have had some great stars. Some have made the Hall of Fame. Who will be the next star?

TEAM FAST FACTS

Founded: 1953 (as the Baltimore Colts)

Home Stadium: Lucas Oil Stadium (Indianapolis, Indiana)

Super Bowl Titles: 2 (1970 and 2006)

NFL Titles: 3 (1958, 1959, and 1968)

Hall of Fame Players: 9, including Gino Marchetti, Raymond Berry, Johnny Unitas, and John Mackey

WORDS TO KNOW

fumble – to drop or lose control of the football

MVP – Most Valuable Player; an honor given to the best player each season

NFL – National Football League; the league pro football players play in

Pro Bowl – the NFL's all-star game

quarterback – a player whose main jobs are to lead the offense and throw passes

rookie – a player in his first season

tackler – a player whose main job is knocking players on the other team to the ground so they cannot score

tight end – a player whose main jobs are to catch passes and block

title – a championship

LEARN MORE

Books

Frisch, Aaron. *Indianapolis Colts*. Mankato, MN: Creative Education, 2011.

Glaser, Jason. *Peyton Manning*. New York: Gareth Stevens, 2012.

Web Sites

Indianapolis Colts—Official Site
http://www.colts.com
Watch video clips and view photos of the Indianapolis Colts.

NFL.com
http://nfl.com
Check out pictures and your favorite football players' stats.

NFL Rush
http://www.nflrush.com
Play games and learn how to be a part of NFL PLAY 60.

INDEX